MIND MELTING

TRIVIA

715 Head Thumpers

that'll Stump Ya!

MIND MELTING
TRIVIA
715 Head Thumpers

that'll Stump Ya!

This book may be ordered by mail from the publisher. Please include $4.95 for postage and handling. Please support your local bookseller first!

Books published by Cider Mill Press Book Publishers are available at special discounts for bulk purchases in the United States by corporations, institutions, and other organizations. For more information, please contact the publisher.

Applesauce Press is an imprint of
Cider Mill Press Book Publishers
"Where good books are ready for press"
12 Port Farm Road
Kennebunkport, Maine 04046

Visit us on the Web!
www.cidermillpress.com

Design by Tilly Grassa, TGCreative Services
Illustrations courtesy of Anthony Owsley
Cover design by Whitney Cookman

Printed in China

1 2 3 4 5 6 7 8 9 0
First Edition

CONTENTS

CHAPTER

Big Screen/Little Screen

1) Match the movie comedy team to their film.

1) The Marx Brothers   a) *Sons of the Desert*

2) Laurel and Hardy   b) *Duck Soup*

3) Abbott and Costello   c) *Buck Privates*

4) Hope and Crosby   d) *The Road to Singapore*

2) TWO MOVIES WERE TIED FOR BEING THE FIRST 3D MOVIES TO BE NOMINATED FOR BEST PICTURE (IN 2009). ONE WAS AN ANIMATED PIXAR MOVIE. THE OTHER WAS A SCIENCE FICTION ADVENTURE. WHAT WERE THEY?

KEVIN!

* *

3) Born in 1954 in Hong Kong, this actor, writer, producer, and director has been called the world's biggest non-Hollywood movie star. Who is this co-star of the remake of *The Karate Kid?*

* *

4) True or false: **Wayne Gretzky** appeared in a *Mighty Ducks* film.

5) **True or false:** Seth Rogan was one of the voices in *Kung Fu Panda*.

****

6> What animal did Angelina Jolie voice in *Kung Fu Panda?*

****

7) True or false: There's a movie called *The Incredibly Strange Creatures Who Stopped Living and Became Mixed-Up Zombies.*

COMPLETE THE TITLES OF THESE FILMS, WHICH ARE ALL PART OF THE NATIONAL FILM REGISTRY.

8) *The Day the Earth Stood _____*

9) *_____ Graffiti*

10) *The Adventures of Robin _____*

11) *The Outlaw Josie _____*

12) *The Life and Times of Rosie the _____*

13) West Side _____

14) _____ and the Beast

15) Young Mr. _____

16) Butch Cassidy and the _____ Kid

17) Seven Brides for Seven _____

18) The Nutty _____

19) Jailhouse _____

20) Going My _____

21) The Rocky Horror Picture ____

22) A Raisin in the _____

23) Miracle on ____ Street

24) The French _____

25) Fast Times at _____ High

26) Cool Hand _____

27) Groundhog _____

28) Blazing _____

29) Wuthering _____

30) The _____ Who Shot Liberty Valance

31) Back to the _____

32) Close Encounters of the Third _____

33) 12 Angry _____

34) The Perils of _____

35) In Cold _____

36) The 7th Voyage of _____

37) The Story of G.I. _____

38) The Muppet _____

39) The Incredible _____ Man

40) Dog Day _____

41) A Tree Grows in _____

42) Saturday Night _____

43) The Pink _____

44) The Empire Strikes _____

45) All the _____ Men

46) _____ X

47) Sunset _____

48) Some Like It ____

49) *Mr. Smith Goes to* _____

50) *The Maltese* _____

51) *High* _____

52) *The Grapes of* _____

53) *Citizen* _____

54) *The Best Years of Our* _____

55) *Rebel Without a* _____

56) *Raging* _____

57) *Duck* _____

58) *Bringing Up* ____

59) *All* ____ *Eve*

60) *The* _____ *of Zenda*

61) *My _____ Clementine*

62) *King _____*

63) *The _____ Rush*

64) *Adam's _____*

65) *A Night at the _____*

66) *Lassie Come _____*

67) *National _____*

68) *_____ of the Sierra Madre*

69) *How Green Was My _____*

70) *The Great Train _____*

71) *All Quiet on the Western _____*

72) *Lawrence of _____*

73) *I Am a Fugitive from a Chain* ____

74) *2001: A Space* _____

75) *Bonnie and* _____

76) *Birth of a* _____

77) *Yankee Doodle* _____

78) True or false: There's a movie called *Operation Dumbo Drop.*

79) Which was made first, *17 Again* or *18 Again.*

80) What letter agent does Will Smith play in the *Men in Black* films?

81) What letter agent does Tommy Lee Jones play in the *Men in Black* films?

82) How many *Back to the Future* movies are there?

COMPLETE THE TITLE OF EACH OF THESE DISNEY CHANNEL ORIGINAL MOVIES.

83) *Full-Court* _____

84) *Cadet* _____

85) *Halloweentown II: Kalabar's* _____

86) *The Luck of the* _____

87) *Phantom of the* _____

88) *Zenon: Girl of the 21st* _____

89) *Harriet the Spy: Blog* _____

90) *16* _____

91) *Den* _____

92) *Phineas and Ferb The Movie; Across the 2nd* _____

93) WERE THERE MORE EPISODES MADE OF *FULL HOUSE* OR *SEINFELD?*

94) Were there more episodes made of *Star Trek: The Next Generation* or *Star Trek?*

95) Were there more episodes made of *Little House on the Prairie* or *The Waltons?*

96) Were there more episodes of *King of the Hill* or *The Flintstones*?

97 > True or false: In the 1980s, a popular Australian kids' TV series was called *Professor Poopsnagle's Steam Zeppelin.*

98) LeVar Burton, the host of *Reading Rainbow*, also starred in a *Star Trek* TV series. Which one?

GOOD NIGHT moon

RED ALER

a) *Star Trek: The Next Generation*
b) *Star Trek* (the original series)
c) *Star Trek: Deep Space Nine*
d) *Star Trek: Voyager*

99) True or false: There was once a TV show called *Monday Night Hockey*.

● ●

100) True or false: **There was once a TV show called *Manimal*.**

101) True or false: There was once a TV show called *Superbrain*.

102) What does O.C. in *The O.C.* stand for?

● ●

103) What does ESPN stand for?

● ●

104) What does CNN stand for?

● ●

105) WHAT DOES TCM STAND FOR?

● ●

106) What does CBS stand for?

107) Match the actress to her show.

1) Alison Brie   a) *2 Broke Girls*

2) Kaley Cuoco   b) *Big Bang Theory*

3) Kat Dennings   c) *Community*

4) Zooey Deschanel   d) *The Middle*

5) Patricia Heaton   e) *New Girl*

108> Match the winner to the show.

1> Fantasia Barrino   a> *So You Think You Can Dance?*

2> Yoanna House

3> Alonzo Boddin   b> *American Idol*

4> Nick Lazzarini   c> *Last Comic Standing*

                     d> *America's Next Top Model*

109) True or false: Alec Baldwin played Mr. Conductor in *Thomas and the Magic Railroad*.

110) The Library of Congress'
National Film Registry selects up
to 25 "culturally, historically
or aesthetically significant films"
each year. Which of the following
was not among the initial group
selected in 1989?
- a) Singin' in the Rain
- b) Star Wars
- c) The Wizard of Oz
- d) Fantasia

111) True or false: *Airplane!* is part of
the National Film Registry.

112) Which of the following was
not in *Get Smart?*
- a) Steve Carell
- b) Nicole Kidman
- c) Anne Hathaway
- d) Alan Arkin

113) Which of the following was not in *Sisterhood of the Traveling Pants?*
a) Amber Tamblyn   b) Alexis Bledel
c) Rose McGowan   d) America Ferrera

114) Which of the following was not in *The Chronicles of Narnia: Prince Caspian?*

   a) George Henley

   b) William Moseley

   c) Anna Popplewell

   d) Emily Blunt

115) Match the cast to the movie.

1) Chris Evans, Hayley Atwell, Tommy Lee Jones

2) Amy Adams, Jason Segal, Chris Cooper

3) James McAvoy, Michael Fassbender, Jennifer Lawrence

4) Logan Lerman, Pierce Brosnan, Sean Bean

5) Christian Bale, Michael Caine, Katie Holmes

6) Eddie Murphy, Raven-Symone, Ossie Davis

a) *X-Men: First Class*

b) *The Muppets*

c) *Captain America: The First Avenger*

d) *Percy Jackson and the Olympians: The Lightening Thief*

e) *Batman Begins*

f) *Dr. Doolittle*

116) TRUE OR FALSE: THERE'S A MOVIE CALLED *BLOOD ON THE BOARDWALK II: PIER PRESSURE.*

117) Which did Jack Black make first, *Nacho Libre* or *Year One?*

CHAPTER

2

Sports

118) IN BASEBALL, FIVE MEN HAVE HIT 60 OR MORE HOMERS IN A SEASON: BABE RUTH, ROGER MARIS, MARK MCGWIRE, SAMMY SOSA, AND BARRY BONDS. PLACE THEM IN ORDER OF HOW MANY CAREER HOMERS THEY HIT.

119) In 2010, what Phillies ace became the second pitcher to throw a postseason no-hitter?
a) Joe Blanton   b) Roy Halladay
c) Cole Hamels   d) Cliff Lee

120) Who threw the only no-hitter in a World Series?
a) Sandy Koufax   b) Don Larsen
c) Allie Reynolds   d) Cy Young

121) Effa Manley is the only woman in the Hall of Fame. What role did she play in the game?
a) Owner   b) Umpire
c) Inventor of the box score and several statistics, including RBI
d) Composer of "Take Me Out to the Ball Game"

122 > What three brothers played the outfield together for two innings in 1963?

   a > Felipe, Matty, and Jesus Alou

   b > Ken, Clete, and Cloyd Boyer

   c > Joe, Dom, and Vince DiMaggio

   d > Ed, Jim, and Tom Delahanty

123) True or false: **Connie Mack managed the A's for 50 years.**

124) Each of these men hit a famous home run to clinch the pennant or World Championship. Which one was not a walk-off homer?

   a) Bobby Thomson   b) Bill Mazeroski

   c) Bucky Dent   d) Joe Carter

125) What pitching feat has been achieved by, among others, Charlie Robertson, Len Barker, Dallas Braden, and David Wells?

★ ★ ★ ★ ★ ★ ★ ★ ★ ★ ★ ★ ★ ★ ★ ★ ★

126) True or false: Hank Aaron and Lou Gehrig have the same first and middle names.

127> Match the nickname to the player:

1> The Count   a> Roger Bresnahan

2> The Duke of Flatbush   b> John Montefusco

3> The Duke of Tralee   c> Babe Ruth

4> The Red Baron   d> Duke Snider

5> The Sultan of Swat   e> Rick Sutcliffe

128) MATCH THE PLAYER TO HIS UNIFORM NUMBER.

1) Mickey Mantle

2) Willie Mays

3) Pete Rose

4) Babe Ruth

a) **3**   b) **7**   c) **14**   d) **24**

★ ★ ★ ★ ★ ★ ★ ★ ★ ★ ★ ★ ★ ★ ★ ★ ★ ★

129) True or false: Babe Ruth once pitched a no-hitter.

HALL OF FAMER, YES OR NO?

130) Elmer Flick?

131) Bill Klem?

132) Dave Parker?

133) Tommy Henrich?

134) Gene Mauch?

135) Eppa Rixey?

136) Bruce Sutter?

137) Ron Santo?

138) Ken Holtzman?

139) Don Drysdale?

140) WHAT PITCHER WON 31 GAMES IN 1968,
THE MOST IN 37 YEARS, BUT ONLY 41 MORE
IN THE REST OF HIS CAREER?
   A) RON BRYANT   B) DON DRYSDALE
   C) BOB GIBSON   D) DENNY MCLAIN

141) **Donora, Pennsylvania,
with a population of less
than 5,000, is nonetheless the
hometown of Ken Griffey
Sr. and Jr., and what Hall of
Famer?**
   a) **Harry Heilmann**
   b) **Stan Musial**
   c) **Al Simmons**
   d) **Willie Stargell**

142) Since 1928, the record for
striking out the most times in a career
has been held in succession by four
Hall of Fame outfielders. Can you
name all four?

143> Which of these cities has never been home to a Major League baseball team?

     a> Altoona, PA

     b> Norfolk, VA

     c> Providence, RI

     d> Toledo, OH

144) Each of these men holds both the single-season and career record in the category given, with one exception. Which one?

a) Barry Bonds, home runs

b) Rickey Henderson, stolen bases

c) Pete Rose, hits

d) Nolan Ryan, strikeouts

* * * * * * * * * * * * * * * * *

145) Who won a batting championship in 1968 with a .301 average, the lowest average ever to win the title?

a) Curt Flood   b) Brooks Robinson

c) Frank Robinson   d) Carl Yastrzemski

146) Who coined the phrase, "It ain't over till it's over"?

    a) Yogi Berra   **b) Dizzy Dean**

    c) Satchel Paige   **d) Casey Stengel**

****

147) True or false: Babe Ruth's real first name was George.

148) Who is the only player to win the batting championship in three different decades?

    a) George Brett   b) Ty Cobb

    c) Tony Gwynn   d) Ted Williams

149) Who was the first National Leaguer to hit 40 homers in a season?

    a) Rogers Hornsby

    b) Stan Musial

    c) Mel Ott

    d) Bill Terry

150) Who was the first National Leaguer to hit 50 homers in a season?
  a) George Foster   b) Ralph Kiner
  c) Willie Mays   d) Hack Wilson

* *

> **151) WHAT IS PRINCE FIELDER'S REAL FIRST NAME?**
>   A) CECIL   B) HENRY
>   C) JADEN   D) PRINCE

* *

152) Who won the first Cy Young Award?

> **153) After his retirement, Jackie Robinson became an executive for what coffee company?**
>   a) Chock Full o' Nuts
>   b) Folger's
>   c) Maxwell House
>   d) Starbucks

154) What Hall of Famer homered in his first career at-bat, and never hit another?

a) Luis Aparicio b) Rabbit Maranville
c) Hoyt Wilhelm d) Cy Young

155> What is the official score of a forfeited game?

a> 1-0   b> 2-0
c> 9-0   d> 0-0

156) True or false: No one is credited as the winning or losing pitcher in a forfeited game.

157) True or false: Statistics from a forfeited game do not count.

158) True or false: a pitcher once retired the side in order for 12 straight innings, and still lost the game.

● ●

159) What nickname was shared by Jim Hunter, Bill Klem, and George Metkovich?
a) Catfish   b) Piano Legs
c) Rabbit   d) Thumper

● ●

160) Place these managers in order of their career wins: Sparky Anderson, Bobby Cox, Leo Durocher, Tony LaRussa, Joe Torre.

161) Who has the most career victories as a manager without ever playing in the majors?
a) Walter Alston
b) Jim Leyland
c) Joe McCarthy
d) Earl Weaver

162) How many Hall of Fame pitchers have losing records?
a) 0   b) 1   c) 2   d) 3

163) WHAT COMEDIAN WAS A COMMENTATOR ON MONDAY NIGHT FOOTBALL FROM 2000-2002?
A) GEORGE CARLIN   B) DENNIS MILLER
C) PETE BARBUTTI   D) JEFF FOXWORTHY

164) How many yards is it from the goal line to the back of the end zone?
a) 5   b) 10   c) 15   d) 17

165) How wide is a football field?
a) 33-1/3 yards
b) 50 yards
c) 53-1/3 yards
d) 66-2/3 yards

166) What school won the first
Rose Bowl?
a) Michigan   b) Ohio State
c) UCLA   d) USC

167 > Match the coach to the school where
he coached the most games.
1 > Bear Bryant   a. Alabama
2 > Woody Hayes   b. Michigan
3 > Joe Paterno   c. Ohio State
4 > Bo Schembechler   d. Penn State

168) How many schools are in the
Big Ten Conference?
a) 8
b) 10
c) 11
d) 12

169) Then Atlanta Falcons' quarterback Michael Vick got in trouble for being involved in what illegal sport?

   a) Bear bating
   b) Cockfighting
   c) Dog fighting
d) Dwarf tossing

WHAT TEAM DID THE FOLLOWING QUARTERBACKS PLAY FOR?

170) Troy Aikman

171) Ken Anderson

172) Terry Bradshaw

173) Tom Brady

174) John Brodie

175) Marc Bulger

176) John Elway

177) Joe Flacco

178) Dan Fouts

179) Josh Freeman

180) David Garrard

181) Pat Haden

182) Eric Hipple

183) Jim Kelly

184) Bill Kenney

185) Neil Lomax

186) Sid Luckman

187) Peyton Manning

188) Dan Marino

189) Matt Ryan

190) Mark Sanchez

191) Phil Simms

192) Brian Sipe

193) Bart Starr

194) Joe Theismann

195) Dave Wilson

196) True or false: The basketball team Buffalo Germans won 111 games in a row from 1908-1911.

197) True or false: No college offered women's varsity basketball until 1950.

198) What basketball position did Bill Russell play?

199) True or false: **Wilt Chamberlain once scored 100 points in a single game.**

200) WHAT COLLEGE TEAM DID JOHN WOODEN COACH FROM 1963-1975?
- A) NYC
- B) UCLA
- C) LSU
- D) USC

201) What position did Oscar Robertson play?

202) What team did Isiah Thomas and Dennis Rodman both play for?

203) What is basketball fandom in Indiana known as?
- a) Hoosier Hoopla
- b) Hoosier Hysteria
- c) Hoosier Hallelujah
- d) Hoosier Hijinks

204 > True or false: **Kareem Abdul-Jabber has the most NBA career games played.**

● ●

205) True or false: Reggie Miller played more NBA games than Julius Erving.

○ ○

206) True or false: Shaquille O'Neal played more NBA games than Moses Malone.

● ●

207) What college did Kobe Bryant play for?

● ● ● ● ● ● ● ● ● ● ● ●

208) What future U.S. senator led Princeton to the Final Four?

209) True or false: Hakeem Olajuwon played more NBA games than Mark Jackson.

- - - - - - -

210) True or false: Elvin Hayes played more NBA games than Karl Malone.

211) True or false: In soccer, Manchester United is based in France.

212) TRUE OR FALSE: DF VALENCIA IS BASED IN BRAZIL.

- - - - - -

213) True or false: Werder Bremen is based in Germany.

- - - - -

214) What are the 1815 rules that helped popularize soccer known as?
a) The Harvard Rules
b) The Oxford Rules
c) The Cambridge Rules
d) The Liverpool Rules

215) True or false: Handling of the soccer ball was banned in 1869.

216> Where was the first World Cup?
  a> Brazil
  b> Uruguay
  c> England
  d> Japan

217) What soccer team has the same name as a U.S. kitchen cleanser and plays at the Amsterdam Arena?

218) Match the hockey team with the city where it used to play.

1) Calgary Flames
2) Carolina Hurricanes
3) Colorado Avalanche
4) Dallas Stars
5) New Jersey Devils
6) Phoenix Coyotes

a) Atlanta
b) Bloomington, Minnesota
c) Denver
d) Hartford
e) Quebec City
f) Winnipeg

* *

219) Which team did Wayne Gretzky never play for?

a) Edmonton Oilers

b) Los Angeles Kings

c) Phoenix Coyotes

d) New York Rangers

220) What arena is home to the New York Rangers?

* * * * * * * * * * * * * * * * * * * *

221) Who is the only person to win the Stanley Cup as a player and an owner?

222) Who was the "Stanley" the Stanley Cup is named for?

a) A player
b) An owner
c) A silversmith
d) A Canadian governor-general

223) There was no winner of the 1919 Stanley Cup. Why not?

a) Flu epidemic
b) Player strike
c) World War I
d) The Cup wasn't created till 1920

* * * * * * * * * * * * * * * * *

224) IN BOXING, WHICH IS HEAVIER: LIGHTWEIGHT OR BANTAMWEIGHT?

225) True or false: In the ancient Greek Olympics, there were no boxing rounds—fighters continued until one was knocked out or gave up.

226) True or false: In 1988, bare-knuckle boxer John L. Sullivan had a match that lasted 75 rounds.

• •

227) True or false: Boxing didn't become a modern Olympic sport until 1964.

• •

228 > In boxing, which is heavier: featherweight or flyweight?

• • • • • • • • • ➤

229) True or false: James II of Scotland banned golf.

• •

230) True or false: The famed St. Andrews Links in Scotland was the first course to have 18 holes.

231) Which of the following is not the name of a course at St. Andrews:

a) Strathtyrum   b) Jubilee

c) Eden   d) McDouglas

232) True or false: Golf was intended to stand for "Gentlemen only, Ladies forbidden."

233) The first golf match to be televised happened in...

a) New York   b) London

c) St. Louis   d) San Francisco

234) Who was the first foreign player to win the Masters?

a) Gary Player   b) Jack Nicklaus

c) Arnold Palmer   d) Mickey Wright

235) What was golf's World Cup called before its name was changed?

    a) Canada Cup
    b) North American Cup
    c) British Cup
    d) None of the above

236) WHAT IS THE MAXIMUM NUMBER OF STROKES FOR A HOLE IN GOLF?

237) True or false: If a golfer gets angry and breaks off the head of a club, he or she can replaced it with a new club during the round.

238) How many clubs is a player allowed to carry in a round?

239) Does an umbrella count as a club carried?

240> What is the maximum number of balls a golfer may carry?

241) Is there a time limit for a golfer to complete a stroke?

242) If all balls are not on the green, who takes the next shot?

243) If a ball falls off a tee before it is hit, does it count as a stroke?

244) What are your choices if the ball you hit accidentally bounces off another player, a caddie, or equipment?

* * * * * * * * * * * * * * * * * *

245) Is a sand trap rake considered a movable obstacle?

* *

246) True or false: Phil Mickelson, who plays left-handed, is really right-handed.

• •

247) The highest golf course in the world is in what country?

a) Tibet
b) Peru
c) Canada
d) Dubai

248) HOW MANY DIMPLES ON A REGULATION GOLF BALL?
A) 150-212
B) 250-289
C) 330-500
D) 550-600

249) True or false: Golf balls used to be packed with pebbles.

****

250) **What month is national golf month?**

****

251) Which of the following is not a layer of a standard golf ball?
a) Polyurethane
b) Synthetic rubber
c) Surlyn
d) Foamcore

252 > Chi Chi Rodriguez was born where?

    a > Guatamala

    b > Chile

    c > Puerto Rico

    d > El Salvador

253) What year did Tiger Woods turn pro?

    a) 1990   b) 1996

    c) 1999   d) 2001

254) What college did Tiger Woods attend?

    a) Stanford

    b) Tufts

    c) University of Maryland

    d) University of Pennsylvania

★ ★ ★ ★ ★ ★ ★ ★ ★ ★ ★ ★ ★ ★ ★ ★

255) What golfer has a lemonade/iced tea drink named after him?

256) Tiger Woods' real first name is:
   a) Earl   b) Eldrick
   c) Vincent   d) Tiger

★ ★ ★ ★ ★ ★ ★ ★ ★ ★ ★ ★ ★ ★ ★ ★ ★

257) The Masters is played in what city?

★ ★ ★ ★ ★ ★ ★ ★ ★ ★ ★ ★ ★ ★ ★ ★ ★

258) Who called golf a good walk spoiled?

   a) Ben Hogan   b) Bobby Jones
   c) Sam Snead   d) Mark Twain

★ ★ ★ ★ ★ ★ ★ ★ ★ ★ ★ ★ ★ ★ ★ ★

259) What color jacket do Masters
champions wear?

★ ★ ★ ★ ★ ★ ★ ★ ★ ★ ★ ★ ★ ★ ★ ★

260) WHAT IS THE TERM FOR SCORING TWO
BELOW PAR ON A HOLE?

261) What is the term for scoring
three below par on a hole?

262) What is the term for scoring
two above par on a hole?

263) What is the term for scoring three above par on a hole?

264> What name is given to a golf round where the purse is divided not based on the number of strokes, but the number of holes won?

265) What French golfer needed only a six on the par-4 18th hole to win the 1999 British Open, but hit shots into the rough and the water to register a seven and lose the tournament in a playoff?

266) What golfer was nicknamed the Shark?

* * * * * * * * * * * * * * *

267) What golfer was nicknamed the Golden Bear?

* *

268) What golfer was nicknamed Super Mex?

* *

269) Who was the youngest player to make an LPGA cut, at age 16?

* *

270) Who has the most wins of any female golfer?

CHAPTER

★ ★ ★ ★ ★ ★ ★ ★ ★ ★

Food for Thought

271) Carbonated water is also called:
   a) Soda water   b) High-fructose water
   c) Waterlite   d) Diet water

272) Carbonated water was developed in...
   a) England   b) France
   c) Germany   d) United States

273) True or false: Cola flavor primarily comes from vanilla and cinnamon.

274 > Was "Make it Real" a Coke or Pepsi slogan?

275) Was "Life Tastes Good" a Coke or Pepsi slogan?

276) Was "It's the Real Thing" a Coke or Pepsi slogan?

277) Was "Generation Next" a Coke or Pepsi slogan?

278) Was "The Choice Is Yours" a Coke or Pepsi slogan?

279) Was "It's the Real Thing" a Coke or Pepsi slogan?

280) Was "You Got the Right One, Baby" a Coke or Pepsi slogan?

281) Was "Catch the Wave" a Coke or Pepsi slogan?

282) TRUE OR FALSE: KOSHER FOR PASSOVER COCA-COLA CONTAINS SUCROSE INSTEAD OF HIGH-FRUCTOSE CORN SYRUP.

283) True or false: In the 1800s, there were three different Coca-Colas on the market.

284) True or false: **The formula for Coca-Cola is in a bank vault.**

285) True or false: The Coca-Cola Company does not produce actual Coca-Cola.

286 > Which came first, Coca-Cola Cherry or Caffeine-Free Coca-Cola?

287) Which came first, Coca-Cola with Lemon or Coca-Cola with Lime?

288) True or false: There was a Coca-Cola Raspberry.

289) True or false: **From the beginning, Coca-Cola was sold in bottles.**

290) True or false: Phosphate soda includes phosphoric acid.

291) True or false: Before 1899, soda bottles were hand blown.

292) When was Coca-Cola invented?
a) 1886   b) 1902   c) 1921   d) 1936

293) When did soda vending machines initially appear.
a) 1900s   b) 1920s   c) 1940s   d) 1960s

294) TRUE OR FALSE: COKE BEGAN BEING SERVED IN CANS IN THE 1930S.

295) True or false: Even though blind taste tests proved tasters preferred New Coke to either Coke or Pepsi, it was still quickly taken off the market.

★ ★ ★ ★ ★ ★ ★ ★ ★ ★ ★ ★ ★ ★ ★ ★

296) What flavor is Mountain Dew Typhoon?

a) Grape

b) Strawberry-pineapple

c) Apple-grape

d) Watermelon

297> What flavor is Mountain Dew Revolution?

a> Wild berry   b> Chocolate
c> Green apple   d> Pomegranate

298) True or false: The nickname Coke wasn't used by the Coca-Cola Company until the 1940s.

299) Which of the following was never a spokesperson for Pepsi products?
a) Michael Jackson   b) Ray Charles
c) Britney Spears   d) Paul McCartney

300) What flavor is Mountain Dew Supernova?
a) White chocolate   b) Strawberry-melon
c) Mango   d) Tangerine

301) What flavor is Diet Mountain Dew Crave?
a) Sweet-and-sour apple b) Banana
c) Mandarin orange   d) Guava

302) True or false: Pink became the standard color of bubble gum in 1952.

★ ★ ★ ★ ★ ★ ★ ★ ★ ★ ★ ★ ★ ★ ★ ★ ★

303) In the movie *Stand By Me*, what flavor Pez does one character say is what he would pick if he could only have one food for the rest of his life?

304) True or false: eBay was created as a way to make Pez-dispenser trading easier.

* * * * * * * * * * *

305) TRUE OR FALSE: IN JAPAN, PEZ CANDY IS WHITE.

* *

306) True or false: the *Oh Henry!* Bar is named for Hank Aaron.

* *

307) True or false: **Baseball great Reggie Jackson once had a candy bar named after him.**

* *

308) What candy bar is named after a novel by Alexandre Dumas?

* *

309> Appropriately, what candy company manufactures the Milky Way bar?

310) What high-end chocolatier is headquartered on San Francisco Bay?
a) Fannie Mae   b) Frango
c) Ghirardelli   d) Godiva

311) What department store produces and distributes Frango mints?
   a) Bloomingdale's b) Filene's
   c) Macy's   d) Neiman-Marcus

312) While several candy bars now have ice cream flavors, what candy bar was an ice cream brand first?
   a) Dove   b) Reese's Pieces
   c) Snickers   d) Symphony

* *

313) What chewing gum has frequently advertised itself using twin sisters as spokesmodels?

314) What candy bar advertised itself as "thickerer"?

a) Chunky b) Dove
c) Marathon d) Whatchamacallit

315) What chocolate company makes Quik instant cocoa?

a) Ghirardelli b) Hershey
c) Mars d) Nestle

316) What provides the crunch in a Nestle Crunch bar?

a) Almonds b) Peanuts
c) Rice d) Walnuts

317) ALTHOUGH THE FIRST LARGE ICE CREAM FACTORY WAS OPEN IN 1851, THE ICE CREAM SCOOP WASN'T SOLD UNTIL...

A) 1860 B) 1897 C) 1912 D) 1929

318) True or false: Peach Melba was named after opera singer Nellie Melba.

319) True or false: **Waldorf Salad was named after Archduke Ferdinand Waldorf.**

320) Which is not a kind of apple?
a) McIntosh   b) Cortland
c) Volcanic   d) Brawley

321) Which is not a kind of pear?
a) Anjou   b) Bartlett
c) Louise   d) Douglas

322) Which is not a kind of cherry?
a) Bigarreau   b) Bing
c) Morello   d) Sultan

323) Which had sushi first, China or Japan?

324) Which of the following is an ingredient in California roll sushi?
a) Pineapple   b) Mango
c) Avocado   d) Peach

325) What is the black seaweed wrap used in some sushi called?

a) Naan   b) Nori   c) Noni   d) Nobi

326) True or false: Soy sauce comes from soybeans.

327) True or false: Avocado is native to Central Australia.

328) Where original quesadilla tortillas made from corn or flour?

329) WHAT DOES "QUESO" MEAN IN SPANISH?

330) True or false: Refried beans are traditionally fried twice.

331) Are traditional Mexican tacos served in U-shaped shells?

332) True or false:
A Virginia Chinese restaurant installed a bulletproof window because it was a favorite place for George W. Bush to eat.

333 > What part of China does Cantonese food come from?
a > North b > South c > East d > West

334) Is Peking Duck considered Beijing cuisine or Sichuan cuisine?

335) Which was not an original flavor of Pop-Tarts?
  a) Strawberry b) Brown sugar cinnamon
  c) Apple currant   d) Cherry

336) Which of the following is not a discontinued variety of Pop-Tarts?
- a) Cheese Danish Pastry Swirls
- b) Frosted Grape
- c) Honey Nut
- d) Hot Chocolate

337) True or false: There wasn't a football player on the front of a Wheaties box until 1986.

338) The first team to appear on a Wheaties box was the...
- a) Minnesota Twins
- b) Chicago Bills
- c) U.S. Olympic basketball team
- d) Philadelphia Flyers

★ ★ ★ ★ ★ ★ ★ ★ ★ ★ ★ ★ ★ ★ ★ ★

339) True or false: A women's sports team has never been on a Wheaties box.

340) Who has been on more different Wheaties boxes: Tiger Woods or Michael Jordan?

341) WHAT KIND OF BIRD IS THE FRUIT LOOPS MASCOT?

342) Match the catchphrase to the fast food chain.
1) Where's the beef?
2) Eat fresh
3) What you crave
4) Home of the Whopper
5) Finger lickin' good
6) Think outside the bun
7) I'm lovin' it.

a) White Castle
b) Burger King
c) Burger King
d) Subway
e) Wendy's
f) Taco Bell
g) McDonald's

343) **Which former Beatle starred in a Pizza Hut commercial?**
a) **John**
b) **Paul**
c) **George**
d) **Ringo**

344) What book is the source of the name "Starbucks"?

345 > On what day do U.S. and Canada 7-Elevens offer free 7.11-ounce Slurpees?

346) True or false: The original Long John Silver's location was in a state without an ocean border.
★★★★★★★★★★★★★★★★★★★★★★

347) What is near the exit of every Long John Silver's restaurant?
★★★★★★★★★★★★★★★★★★★★★★

348) What are the deep-fried cornmeal balls served at Long John Silver's called?
✳ ✳

349) True or false: The original Long John Silver's location is now a McDonald's.

350) True or false: According to one study, the average sandwich at the Cheesecake Factory contained almost 1,400 calories.

351) True or false: Outback Steakhouse was founded in Texas.

* *

352) True or false: There are no Outback Steakhouses in Australia.

* *

353) TRUE OR FALSE: THERE ARE MORE THAN 100 OUTBACK STEAKHOUSES IN SOUTH KOREA.

* *

354) Did the first Big Boy restaurant launch before or after World War II?

355) What are the two colors on the Big Boy overalls?

356) True or false: There are more than 150 Big Boy Japan restaurants.

* *

357 > True or false: Before 1984, Shoney's featured the Big Boy statue.

358) True or false: There was an *Adventures of Big Boy* comic book.

359) What color, traditionally, are the roofs of Howard Johnson's?

360) Which came first, Howard Johnson's restaurants or hotels?

361) What is traditionally on top of a Howard Johnson's restaurant?

362) True or false: There were once HoJos Campgrounds.

363) True or false: It is against government standards to include vinegar in ketchup.

364) TRUE OR FALSE: KETCHUP CAN BE USED TO SHINE GOLD.

• •

365) True or false: Topps first combined baseball cards and bubble gum in 1971.

366) Match the slogan to the candy.
1) Gimme a break   a) Almond Joy
2) The Great American   b) Hershey's
   Chocolate Bar   c) Kit Kat
3) Melts in your mouth,   d) M&M's
   not in your hand
4) Sometimes you feel like a nut

367) Not counting special promotions, what color M&M was most recently added, in 1995?

• •

368) What candy was prominently featured in the movie "E.T."?

369 > Bart Simpson has appeared in commercials for what candy bar?

370) True or false: Pez comes from the German word Phefferminz

371) True or false: From the time it was launched, Pez candies included a dispenser.

372) The first Pez dispenser sold in America featured what on top?
   a) A Ford automobile
   b) A Mickey Mouse head
   c) Santa Claus
   d) The White House

373) The chocolate-covered ice cream bar, the Eskimo Pie, was launched in 1934 in the city of Onawa. What state is Onawa in?
a) Ohio b) Indiana c) Iowa d) Idaho

374) True or false: Haagen-Dazs is a Danish company.

375) Ice cream and frozen custard each contain about what percentage of butterfat?
a) 2%   b) 10%   c) 15%   d) 21%

376) Sherbet contains about what percentage of butterfat?
a) 1-2%   b) 3-4%   c) 5-6%   d) 7-8%

377) THE MAN WHO CREATED THE FIRST CHOCOLATE BAR WAS FROM...
A) ENGLAND   B) FRANCE
C) SWITZERLAND   D) CHINA

378) In what year did the F. & J. Heinz Company start marketing ketchup?
a) 1744   b) 1876   c) 1902   d) 1929

379) True or false:
The flowers of a mustard plant are not edible.

380) Bordeaux mustard is made with...

a) Cheese   b) Dough

c) Tomato   d) Grape juice

★ ★ ★ ★ ★ ★ ★ ★ ★ ★ ★ ★ ★ ★ ★ ★

381 > True or false: The mustard most used on hot dogs, American mustard or yellow mustard, was actually created in Egypt.

★ ★ ★ ★ ★ ★ ★ ★ ★ ★ ★ ★ ★ ★ ★ ★

382) Are anchovies a salt-water or fresh-water fish?

★ ★ ★ ★ ★ ★ ★ ★ ★ ★ ★ ★ ★ ★ ★ ★

383) True or false: Anchovies have no teeth.

★ ★ ★ ★ ★ ★ ★ ★ ★ ★ ★ ★ ★ ★ ★ ★

384) True or false: Pizza Hut and Red Roof Inn are owned by the same company.

★ ★ ★ ★ ★ ★ ★ ★ ★ ★ ★ ★ ★ ★ ★ ★

385) True or false: Church's Chicken was so named because the first restaurant was housed in a former church.

386) True or false: During the time it was owned by an Islamic venture capital firm, all pork products were removed from the Church's Chicken menu.

★ ★ ★ ★ ★ ★ ★ ★ ★ ★ ★ ★ ★ ★ ★ ★

387) Which of the following is not a Church's Chicken side dish?
  a) Collard Greens   b) Okra
  c) Mini-wings   d) Sweet Corn Nuggets

388) Which of the following is not a sauce available at Church's Chicken?
  a) White Gravy   b) Cocktail Sauce
  c) Creamy Jalapeno Sauce   d) Tarter Sauce

389) What is the name of Cap'n Crunch's ship?
  a) Goldfish   b) Guppy
  c) Minnow   d) Squid

390) True or false: A toy whistle included as a prize in boxes of Cap'n Crunch could be used to make long-distance phone calls for free.

• •

391) WHAT KIND OF CREATURE IS THE MASCOT FOR PEANUT BUTTER CRUNCH?

• •

392) What pirate is constantly trying to steal Cap'n Crunch?

393) What animator created the Cap'n Crunch characters?
a) Tex Avery   b) Matt Groening
c) Chuck Jones   d) Jay Ward

394) What hot cereal's slogan was the basis for the later slogan, "I want my MTV"?

a) Cream of Wheat   b) Maypo
c) Postum   d) Quaker Oats

395 > What cereal, now a generic term, debuted at the Chicago World's Fair in 1893?

a > Corn flakes   b > Grape nuts
c > Raisin bran   d > Shredded wheat

• •

396) Which has more calories, peaches or prunes?

• •

397) Which has more calories, papaya or passion fruit?

• •

398) Which has more calories, green pepper or red pepper?

• •

399) Which has more calories, onion or parsley?

• •

400) Which has more calories, pumpkin or peas?

CHAPTER

4

★★★★★★★★★★

401) What tells you how many spaces to move in Chutes and Ladders?

   a) Dice
   b) Tiles
   c) A spinner
   d) None of
      the above

• • • • • • • • • • • •

402) How many peg spaces are there in Battleship's submarine piece?

403> How many peg spaces are there in a Battleship's aircraft carrier piece?

404) True or false: The 2010 updated version of Battleship includes islands.

• •

405) True or false: Blue box Boggle contains the same number of Ks as yellow box Boggle.

406) How many cards do you draw at the beginning of a basic game of Pokémon?

407) How many different shapes are there in a game of Qwirkle?

408) How many monkeys do you need to hook together to win a game of Barrel of Monkeys?

409) True or false: Chutes and Ladders is based on an Indian game called Snakes and Ladders.

410) True or false: The spaces in Chutes and Ladders are lettered.

411) WHAT IS THE HIGHEST NUMBER OF DOTS ON ONE STANDARD DOMINO?

412) True or false: **More than 1,000,000 dominoes were set up and toppled by one person in Singapore in 2003.**

413) True or false: Dominoes are sometimes called bones.

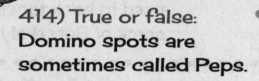

414) True or false: Domino spots are sometimes called Peps.

415 > What is the highest number on a backgammon doubling cube?

POINK!

416) If the loser of a game of backgammon still has a checker in the winner's home board, is that a gammon or a backgammon?

417) Are the players in Apples to Apples dealt green apple cards or red apple cards?

418) Are there more red or green cards in Apples to Apples?

419) What is the Cranium version for kids called?

420) True or false: There's a game called Cranium Kabookii.

421) True or false: There's a game called Cranium Brainbuster.

422) Is the game Landslide about natural disasters or presidential politics?

423) What does it say on a Mouse Trap space that would require a player to start operating the trap?

★ ★

424) WHICH COMES FIRST IN MOUSE TRAP, THE DIVER OR THE MARBLE?

★ ★

425) True or false: Scene It was originally played with Super 8 movie film.

★ ★

426) Which is not a part of your character's Dungeons and Dragons ability score:

a) Strength   b) Fortitude
c) Wisdom   d) Charisma

★ ★

427) In the first edition of Dungeons and Dragons, which of the following was not a player class:

a) Monk b) Bard   c) Cleric d) Leader

★ ★

428 > Which of the following was not a core race in the original Dungeons and Dragons:

a > Elf   b > Gnome c > Sprite d > Dwarf

429) In Dungeons and Dragons, what is a D20?

★ ★ ★ ★ ★ ★ ★ ★ ★ ★

430) How many A tiles are there in a game of Scrabble?

★ ★ ★ ★ ★ ★ ★ ★ ★ ★ ★ ★ ★ ★ ★ ★ ★ ★

431) True or false: Scrabble's original name was Lexicogs.

★ ★ ★ ★ ★ ★ ★ ★ ★ ★ ★ ★ ★ ★ ★ ★ ★

432) True or false: Scrabble's creator was named Alfred Butts.

I SAID NO PROPER NOUNS!

★ ★ ★ ★

433) True or false: The same inventor created a game called Alfred's Other Game.

434) True or false: There is no Scrabble-acceptable two-letter word containing a V.

* *

435) IN SCRABBLE, ARE THERE MORE PS OR US?

* *

436) In Scrabble, are there more Ys or Gs?

* * * * * * * * * * * * * * * * *

437) Are there any acceptable Scrabble words containing a Q but no U?

* * * * * * * * * * * * * *

438) How many letters are represented just once in a Scrabble set?

* * * * * * * * * * * * * * * *

439> What color piece is Mrs. Peacock in Clue?

* * * * * * * * * * * * * * *

440) True or false: In some editions of Clue the rope is made of string. In others, it's plastic.

441) Which is not a room in Clue:

a) Dining Room   b) Laundry Room

c) Kitchen   d) Conservatory

442) How many possible murderer/location/weapon combinations are there in a standard game?

a) 124   b) 196   c) 224   d) 324

443) True or false: The guy in Monopoly jail doesn't have an official name.

* * * * * * * * * * * * * * * * * * * *

444) True or false: In France, the Boardwalk space has been replaced with the Eiffel Tower.

* *

445) True or false: Escape maps were hidden in Monopoly sets that were sent to American prisoners or war during World War II.

GET OUT OF JAIL FREE!

446) WHICH OF THE FOLLOWING WAS NOT
ONCE A MONOPOLY PIECE:
    A) LANTERN   B) PURSE
    C) SLED   D) ROCKING HORSE

447) Was the dog one of the original
Monopoly pieces?

448) Was the wheelbarrow one of the
original Monopoly pieces?

449) In what movie do characters play
Monopoly with real money?
    a) *Night of the Living Dead*
    b) *Zombieland*
    c) *Shaun of the Dead*
    d) *Return of the Living Dead*

450 > True or false: The prize at the
Monopoly World Championships is the real dollar
equivalent of the amount of fake money in a
Monopoly game box.

451) How many houses in a Monopoly game?

452) What color are the $20 bills?

453) What color are the $1 bills?

454) Can you buy property while you are in jail?

455) Which of the following can't you do with a Monopoly speed dice, introduced in 2007?

a) Move three additional spaces

b) Move to the next unowned property

c) Buy an undeveloped property from another player for the face value

d) Opt to use just one of the die and "get off the bus early"

456) True or false: **Monopoly was banned in the Soviet Union as capitalistic.**

457) HOW MUCH DO YOU GET FOR SELLING A GET OUT OF JAIL FREE CARD BACK TO THE BANK?

458) How many Monopoly properties are named after saints?

• •

459) True or false: if you land on Go instead of passing it, you get $400, not $200.

• •

460) Which property completes the monopoly if you own St. Charles Place and Virginia Ave.?

• •

461> Which property completes the monopoly if you own Marvin Gardens and Atlantic Ave.?

• • • • • • • • • • • •

462) True or false: Many 1,000-piece jigsaw puzzles actually have more than 1,000 pieces.

...AND SOMETIMES LESS!

463) In a crossword puzzle, what is used to indicate that the clue indicates a pun?

464) When was the first crossword puzzle published?
   a) 1654   b) 1712   c) 1890   d) 1910

465) True or false: The oldest jigsaw puzzle—then called a dissected puzzle—was created by a Japanese toymaker.

466) True or false: Romans sometimes used coconuts to play an early version of bocce.

467) True or false: King Carlos IV of Spain is the only king to prohibit bocce playing.

468) How many games in a bocce match?

469) TRUE OR FALSE: IN CHAMPIONSHIP BOCCE, THREE PLAYERS ON EACH TEAM PLAY THE ENTIRE MATCH.

470) Championship bocce games usually go to how many points?

★ ★

471) True or false: **The Atari was the first home video game system.**

★ ★ ★ ★ ★

472) Atari is a term used when playing Parcheesi.

VIDEO GAME PRESERVE

★ ★

473> Who was the exclusive seller of Atari's Pong game?

a> Wal-Mart   b> K-Mart

c> Sears   d> Macy's

★ ★ ★ ★ ★ ★ ★ ★ ★ ★ ★ ★ ★ ★ ★ ★ ★ ★ ★ ★

474) What year did Space Invaders first invade arcades?

a) 1976   b) 1978   c) 1980   d) 1982

475) Which came
first, Asteroids
or Pac-man?

★ ★ ★ ★ ★ ★ ★

476) The Nintendo
Entertainment
System was first
known as:

a) Famicom   b) Gencon

c) Playcom   d) Gamicon

477) What is the name of
the addictive game developed by Russian
programmer Alex Pajitnov in 1985?

478) What year was
the Nintendo Game Boy first released?

a) 1986   b) 1989   c) 1991   d) 1993

★ ★ ★ ★ ★ ★ ★ ★ ★ ★ ★ ★ ★ ★

479) True or false: The Entertainment Software
Ratings Board began in 1989, the same year that
the Sega Genesis system was launched.

480) The highest possible score in Pac-man is:

    a) 1,010,101   b) 1,111,120

    c) 2,222,240   d) 3,333,360

* * * * * * * * * * * * * * *

    481) WHICH CAME FIRST, THE SIMS OR TAMAGOTCHI?

* * * * * * * * * * * * * * *

482) Which came first Sony PSP or Nintendo's Wii?

* * * * * * * * * * * * * * * * * * * *

483) True or false: **Super Mario Bros. is a spin-off from the game Donkey Kong.**

* * * * * * * * * * * * * * *

484) Which came first, Super Mario World or Super Mario Bros. 3?

* * * * * * * * * * * * * * *

485 > For what computer was the first John Madden Football game designed?

486) True or false: The original Guitar Hero was released for Playstation I.

* *

487) Which of the following is not a song on the main set list of the first Rock Band?

    a) "Ballroom Blitz"
    b) "Philadelphia Freedom"
    c) "Suffragette City"
    d) "Won't Get Fooled Again"

* * * * * * * * * * * * * *

488) Which of the following artists does not have a hit song of his or hers featured on the first Rock Band?

    a) Red Hot Chili Peppers
    b) Kiss
    c) Madonna
    d) The Police

SONG NOT — FOUND —

* * * * * *

489) What two colors are the arrow footpads on the standard Dance Dance Revolution arcade game?

490) Which came first, Myst or Halo?

491) True or false: A 1982 song called "Pac-Man Fever" actually became a top-10 record.

492) What color is Pac-Man?

493) WHERE DO THE SIMS LIVE?

494) True or false: In the first Sims game, children did not grow up into adults.

495) True or false: After a Sim dies, it may haunt the place where its life ended.

****

496) True or false: When it was released, the Sims became the bestselling game in PC history.

497> What language do Sims speak?

498) Which expansion came first: The Sims: Superstar or The Sims: Hot Date?

499) What game sold more copies for Atari, Missile Command or Pac-Man?

• •

500) Which sold more copies for Wii: Wii Fit or Mario Party 8?

• •

501) Which sold more for PlayStation: Tomb Raider II or Tom Raider?

502) Which sold more for PlayStation 2: Final Fantasy X or Grand Theft Auto III?

503) True or false: Over $2.5 billion in quarters were spent in Pac-Man video games.

504) What was the code name for the Wii while it was in development?
a) Reaction   b) Revolution
c) Recreator   d) Recreationator

505) TRUE OR FALSE: THE WII WAS AVAILABLE IN WHITE, BLUE, OR RED IN ITS FIRST YEAR.

506) Which sold more for Wii: Wii Party or Wii Play?

COMPLETE THE TITLE OF THESE WII GAMES:

507) Active Life: Extreme _____

508) Alien _____ Bowling League

509) AMF Bowling World _____

510) Are You Smarter Than a 5th Grader:

   Make the ____

511) Backyard Sports: Sandlot _____

512) Batman: The Brave and the _____

513) Big Brain _____: Wii Degree

514) Bratz: Girlz Really _____!

515) Cabela's Big Game _____

516) Call of Duty: Black ____

517) Celebrity Sports _____

518) Doctor Fizzwhizzle's Animal _____

519) Donkey Kong Jungle _____

520) Kidz Bop Dance _____

521) Kirby's Return to _____

522) Legend of Zelda; Skyward _____

523) Mario and Sonic at the _____ Games

524) MySims: Sky _____

525) Pet Pals: Animal _____

526) Pirates vs. _____: Dodgeball

527) Which of the following is not a
Super Mario game for Wii?
   a) Super Mario Galaxy 2
   b) Super Mario All-Stars
   c) Super Paper Mario
   d) Super Mario Indestructible

528) **Which of the following is not a Tony Hawk game for Wii?**
  a) Tony Hawk's Downhill Jam
  b) Tony Hawk: Shred
  c) Tony Hawk: Ride It Alone
  d) Tony Hawk's Proving Ground

529) Which Wii game was released first in the U.S., Super Swing Golf or Madden NFL 07?

530 > Which Wii game was released first in the U.S., Brunswick Pro Bowling or MySims?

531) Which came first for Wii, LEGO Indiana Jones: The Original Adventures or LEGO Star Wars: The Complete Saga.

532) Which came first for Wii: LEGO Batman or LEGO Harry Potter?

* * * * * * * * * * * * * *

533) The designer of Angry Birds is from:
    a) England
    b) Finland
    c) Congo
    d) Ecuador

* *

534) In Angry Birds, what is a player trying to hit with the birds?

535) What color are the birds at the initial levels of Angry Birds?

536) How many smaller birds can the blue bird separate into in Angry Birds?

537) What does a white bird drop in Angry Birds?

538) HOW MANY LEVELS IN EACH CHAPTER OF THE INITIAL RELEASE OF ANGRY BIRDS?

539) True or false: Rovio, maker of Angry Birds, also made the game Desert Sniper?

540) What is the name of the player character in Portal?

a) Krell   b) Chell

c) Shell   d) Mell

● ●

541) What is the player character in Portal promised as a prize when all of the puzzles are solved?

● ●

542 > True or false: The Legend of Zelda was originally released as the Hyrule Fantasy: Legend of Zelda.

● ●

543) In Zelda, how many fragments of the Triforce of Wisdom must be collected?

● ●

544) Who is the villain of The Legend of Zelda?

a) Ganon   b) Gamon

c) Gambon   d) Grammion

545) True or false: Zelda takes place in the land of Hyrule.

• •

What video game do these villains come from?

546) Mother Brain

547) Dr. Robotnik

548) Joker

549) Ganon

550) Bowser

CHAPTER

5

Mother Earth

551) Which is closer to the Earth's surface, the mantle or the outer core?

552) ABOUT HOW DEEP IS THE EARTH'S CRUST?
　　A) 2 MILES　　B) 4 MILES
　　C) 10 MILES　　D) 25 MILES

553) About how deep is the Earth's magma layer?
　　a) 100 miles　b) 1,000 miles
　　c) 1,800 miles　d) 2,400 miles

● ●

554) True or false: The Earth's inner core is estimated to be about the size of the Moon.

● ●

555) About how many different kinds of minerals are there on Earth?
　　a) 1,000　　b) 1,200
　　c) 1,500　　d) 2,000

● ●

556> About how much shorter are mountains estimated to get every 1,000 years?
　　a> 30 feet　　b> 3 feet
　　c> 30 inches　　d> 3 inches

557) What is between topsoil and bedrock?
   a) Subsoil
   b) Midsoil
   c) Secondary soil
   d) Lightsoil

●●●●●●●●●●●●●●●●●●●●●●●●●●●

558) What discovery helped date the age of the Earth?

a) Gravity
b) Radioactivity
c) Nuclear power
d) Atomic power

●●●●●●●●●●●●●●●●●●●●●●●●●●●

559) Which period in Earth's history came first, the Priscoan or the Archean?

●●●●●●●●●●●●●●●●●●●●●●●●●●●

560) True or false: The ozone layer developed during the Proterozoic period.

561) What is the equatorial circumference of the Earth?
   a) About 24,000 miles
   b) About 32,000 miles
   c) About 40,000 miles
   d) About 48,000 miles

562) True or false: It's calculated that the Earth reverses its polarity every half a million years.

563) Does the Earth contain more magnesium or sodium?

564) DOES THE EARTH CONTAIN MORE ALUMINUM OR POTASSIUM?

565) Does the Earth contain more silicon or iron?

566) True or false: Earthquakes come before all volcano eruptions.

567) Which is not one of the places where you can find a geyser.
a) United States   b) Ethiopia
c) Spain   d) Chile

568> Everest is called Sagarmatha in Nepalese. What does that mean?
a> King of the mountains
b> King of the heavens
c> King of the hills
d> King of the Earth

569) How many of the 14 "eight-thousanders" (mountains over 8,000 meters high) are located in the Himalayas?

• •

570) From what country was the first woman to reach Everest's peak?
   a) England   b) Thailand
   c) Japan   d) Australia

• •

571) True or false: Snow slides are often deliberately caused on mountains in order to avoid future avalanches.

572) About what percent of the land mass of the Earth is covered in ice?
a) 5%   b) 10%   c) 15%   d) 20%

573) What is the only continent without mountain glaciers?

• •

574) Which is more likely to have some trees, a veldt or a plain?

575) About how much of an iceberg is typically above the water level?

a) One-quarter   b) One-half

c) One-sixth   d) One-ninth

576) TRUE OR FALSE: THE FIZZING SOUND A MELTING ICEBERG MAKES IS KNOWN AS "BERGIE SELTZER."

577) Which is larger, a medium or a growler iceberg?

578) Which is larger, a Bergy Bit or a small iceberg?

579) True or false: George Everest was the first person to reach the top of the mountain that would be named after him.

580 > What percentage of the Earth is covered by water?

a > 48%   b > 63%   c > 71%   d > 82%

581) Which ocean has the most islands?

582) Is the average depth of the Pacific Ocean over or under 10,000 feet?

583) Is the deepest part of the Pacific Ocean more or less than 35,000 feet?

584) Is the deepest part of the Atlantic Ocean more or less than 35,000 feet?

585) Is the deepest part of the Indian Ocean more or less than 30,000 feet?

586) How many square miles is the Indian Ocean?

    a) 15 million   b) 20 million

    c) 29 million   d) 43 million

587) What is the average salt content of the oceans?
a) 1% b) 3.5% c) 4.8% d) 6%

588) TRUE OR FALSE: THE HOTTER AND DRYER THE CLIMATE, THE GREATER THE SALT CONTENT IN THE OCEAN.

****

589) In the open sea, about how far can sunlight reach underwater?
a) 1,280 feet
b) 2,480 feet
c) 3,280 feet
d) 4,680 feet

****

590) True or false: The unit used to measure ocean current is the sverdrup.

****

591) Where are the strongest tidal currents found?
a) Florida's Atlantic coast
b) Japan's Pacific coast
c) Finland
d) Chile

592 > About how long is the U.S. continental coastline?

a > 100,000 miles   b > 200,000 miles

c > 250,000 miles   d > 350,000 miles

593) How high do most waves get?
a) About 4 feet b) About 6 feet
c) About 8 feet d) About 10 feet

594) True or false: About half of the world's population lives within 60 miles of an ocean.

****

595) Is the Atlantic Ocean growing or shrinking?

****

596) True or false: A 100-year flood is a flood that happens every 100 years.

****

597) In what state is Siesta Beach considered by some to be the best beach in the U.S.?

598) In what state are Wildwood, North Wildwood, and Wildwood Crest beaches?

599) In what state is Kauapea Beach?

600) IN WHAT STATE IS OCRACOKE ISLAND BEACH?

601) In what state is Wildcat Beach?

602) True or false:
New Smyrna Beach is right next to Old Smyrna Beach.

603) In what state is Poipu Beach?

604 > In what state is Sanibel Island?

605) In what state is South Padre Island?

606) In what state is Catalina Island?

607) In what New England State is Old Orchard Beach?

608) In what Pacific state is Cannon Beach?

609) The ancient Egyptians called the Nile River Ar, which means what?
- a) Water
- b) Black
- c) Flowing
- d) Danger

610) Is the Nile shorter or longer than 4,000 miles?

611) True or false: **The Nile touches Ethiopia, Kenya, and Zaire.**

612) TRUE OR FALSE: THERE ARE NO CROCODILES IN THE NILE.

613) Which has a higher average discharge of water, the Amazon or the Nile?

614) True or false: **During the wet season, the Amazon can be 40 miles wide.**

★ ★ ★ ★ ★ ★ ★ ★ ★ ★ ★ ★ ★ ★ ★ ★

615) True or false: No bridges cross the Amazon.

★ ★ ★ ★ ★ ★ ★ ★ ★ ★ ★ ★ ★ ★ ★ ★

616 > Which of the following does the Amazon not flow through.

a > Brazil   b > Colombia

c > Chile   d > Bolivia

★ ★ ★ ★ ★ ★ ★ ★ ★ ★ ★ ★ ★ ★ ★ ★

617) Does the Amazon end farther east than its beginning or farther west?

618) True or false: There are piranhas in the Amazon River.

619) Which is larger, a channel or a sound?

620) The Cuyahoga River in Ohio was so polluted that it caught fire.

★ ★ ★ ★ ★ ★ ★

621) Mount Everest is the Earth's highest mountain. Which side of the Nepal/Chinese border is it on?

★ ★ ★ ★ ★ ★ ★ ★ ★ ★ ★ ★ ★ ★ ★ ★

622) True or false: The Appalachians stretch from Quebec to Alabama.

623) On what continent are the Andes?

624) ON WHAT CONTINENT IS THE HAMERSLEY RANGE?

★ ★ ★ ★ ★ ★ ★ ★ ★ ★ ★ ★ ★ ★ ★ ★

625) On what continent are the Jura Mountains?

★ ★ ★ ★ ★ ★ ★ ★ ★ ★ ★ ★ ★ ★ ★ ★

626) On what continent are the San Bernardino Mountains?

627) On what continent are the Kunlun Mountains?

CHAPTER

6

Disney

628) PUT THESE FIVE EARLY DISNEY MOVIES IN ORDER OF THEIR FIRST THEATRICAL RELEASE.

PINOCCHIO
DUMBO
BAMBI
SNOW WHITE AND THE SEVEN DWARFS
FANTASIA

629) In *Beauty and the Beast*, what is the name of the clock?

630) In *Beauty and the Beast*, what is Belle's father's invention supposed to do?

631) What is Gaston "especially good at"?

632 > Who is Chip's mother?

633) True or false: *Beauty and the Beast* lost the Best Picture Academy Award to *Dances with Wolves*.

634) What color is Belle's dress she wears while in town?

635) **True or false:** *Beauty and the Beast* **begins with the words "Once upon a time."**

636) How many times did the Prince dismiss the beggar woman?

637) The rose was enchanted to bloom until the Prince's _____ birthday?

638) Who wrote the original story of The Little Mermaid?

    a) *The Brothers Grimm*

    b) *Hans Christian Anderson*

    c) *Edger Allen Poe*

    d) *H.G. Wells*

639) What song from *The Little Mermaid* won the Academy Award for Best Song?

640) WHO SAYS THAT THE PRINCE IN *THE LITTLE MERMAID* LOOKS "KINDA HAIRY AND SLOBBERY"?

641) For how many days does the potion turn Ariel into a human?

642) What exactly is the thing that gets called a "dinglehopper"?

643) True or false: A man voiced Ursula, the sea witch, in *The Little Mermaid.*

644> What is the name of the human that Ursula transforms into?

645) What is the name of the mouse in *Dumbo?*

646) True or false: Dumbo was supposed to be on the cover of *Time* magazine in December of 1941 but that changed when Pearl Harbor was bombed.

647) Does Dumbo ever talk?

648) True or false: In Disney's *Cinderella,* the stepsisters are named Drizella and Ariella.

649) True or false: In Disney's *Cinderella,* the prince is never named.

650) Which song comes first in Disney's *Peter Pan,* "The Second Star to the Right" or "A Pirate's Life"?

651) In the Disney film, which hand of Captain Hook's is a hook, left or right?

* * * * * * * * * * *

652) WHAT ARE LADY AND TRAMP EATING WHEN "BELLA NOTTE" IS SUNG TO THEM?

* *

653) True or false: The Siamese cats in *Lady and the Tramp* are named Si and Am.

* *

654) In Disney's *Sleeping Beauty,* the title character is named Aurora. Is this her name in the German or the Italian version of the story?

655) In *The Fox and the Hound,* is Copper the fox or the hound?

****

656 > Is Vixey a fox or a hound?

****

657) How many kittens does Duchess have in *The Aristocats?*

658) True or false: The same actor voiced Thomas O'Malley in *The Aristocats*, Baloo the Bear in *Jungle Book*, and Little John in *Robin Hood*.

659) True or false: *Tangled* was originally going to be called *Rapunzel Unbraided.*

* * * * * * * * * * * * * * *

660) What is the hero's name in *Tangled?*

    a) Flint Riser   b) Flynn Rider
    c) Frank Rymer   d) Fred Reisler

661) True or false: Randy Newman wrote the songs for *Tangled*.

662) Disney's *The Princess in the Frog* is set in the...
a) 1880s
b) 1920s
c) 1940s
d) 1960s

663) **Which of the following is not a character in *Brother Bear?***
a) Koda
b) Kenai
c) Sitka
d) Sakina

664) WHO IS THE FATHER OF *HERCULES?*

665) How many of Greek mythology's nine muses were used in Disney's *Hercules?*

666) True or false: Susan Egan, who played the voice of Meg in Disney's *Hercules*, played Belle in Broadway's *Beauty and the Beast.*

667) True or false: in *Hercules*, Zeus' voice was created by computer and didn't use an actor.

• •

668 > What are the names of the two evil minions of *Ares in Hercules?*

　a > Pain and Pleasure
　b > Pain and Panic
　c > Mean and Nasty
　d > Hurt and Help

• •

IT'S GREAT BEING HERE TONIGHT, DAVE!

669) Paul Shaffer, who played the voice of Hermes in *Hercules,* is bandleader for what late night TV show?

670) Hercules' Roman numeral credit card says it expires in the year M BC. What year is that?

671) **What is Hercules' flying horse's name?**

672) True or false: The talking statues in Disney's *The Hunchback of Notre Dame* were named after the author of the original novel?

673) Which songs comes earlier in *The Hunchback of Notre Dame*: "God Help the Outcasts" or "A Guy Like You"?

674) True or false: Belle from *Beauty and the Beast* makes a brief appearance in The Hunchback of Notre Dame.

675) Stephen Schwartz wrote the music and lyrics for Disney's *The Hunchback of Notre Dame*. He also wrote the music and lyrics for a hit Broadway show about a witch. Name it.

676) TRUE OR FALSE: IN THE *LION KING*, ZAZU HAS A DIFFERENT NUMBER OF TAIL FEATHERS DEPENDING ON THE SCENE.

677) True or false: Elton John was an unknown songwriter when he wrote the score for *The Lion King*.

678) True or false: The same actor who voices adult Simba in *The Lion King* also starred in the movie Inspector Gadget.

679) James Earl Jones, who provided the voice for Mufasa in *The Lion King* also provided the voice for a villain in a non-animated film series. Name the series.

I AM YOUR FATHER!

WHAT MOVIES DO THESE VILLAINS COME FROM?

****

681 > Cruella de Vil

****

682 > Dr. Facilier

****

683 > Frollo

****

684 > Gaston

****

685 > Hades

****

686 > Jafar

****

687 > Madame Medusa

698) What kind of cats menace Lady and the Tramp?

699) **What is the last name of the family befriended by Peter Pan?**

700) What does Wendy sew back together for Peter Pan?

701) What is Sleeping Beauty's real name?

702) What is the name of the Lion King at the beginning of the movie?

703) **By the end of the movie, who is the new Lion King?**

704) IN THE DISNEY VERSION OF *ROBIN HOOD,* WHAT KIND OF ANIMAL IS ROBIN HOOD?

705) What is the name of the mouse in *Dumbo?*

NAME EACH OF THESE DISNEY PRINCESS'S TRUE LOVE.

706) Ariel

707) Aurora

708) Cinderella

709) Esmeralda

710) Jazmine

711) Meg

712) Nala

713) Pocahontas

714) Tiana

715) Vixen

ANSWERS

1) 1 b, 2 a, 3 c, 4 d
2) *Up* and *Avatar*
3) Jackie Chan
4) true
5) true
6) a tiger
7) true
8) *Still*
9) *American*
10) *Hood*
11) *Wales*
12) *Riveter*
13) *Story*
14) *Beauty*
15) *Lincoln*
16) *Sundance*
17) *Brothers*
18) *Professor*
19) *Rock*
20) *Way*
21) *Show*
22) *Sun*
23) *34th*
24) *Connection*

25) *Ridgemont*
26) *Luke*
27) *Day*
28) *Saddles*
29) *Heights*
30) *Man*
31) *Future*
32) *Kind*
33) *Men*
34) *Pauline*
35) *Blood*
36) *Sinbad*
37) *Joe*
38) *Movie*
39) *Shrinking*
40) *Afternoon*
41) *Brooklyn*
42) *Fever*
43) *Panther*
44) *Back*
45) *King's*
46) *Malcolm*
47) *Boulevard*
48) *Hot*

49) *Washington*
50) *Falcon*
51) *Noon*
52) *Wrath*
53) *Kane*
54) *Lives*
55) *Cause*
56) *Bull*
57) *Soup*
58) *Baby*
59) *About*
60) *Prisoner*
61) *Darling*
62) *Kong*
63) *Gold*
64) *Rib*
65) *Opera*
66) *Home*
67) *Velvet*
68) *Treasure*
69) *Valley*
70) *Robbery*
71) *Front*
72) *Arabia*

73) *Gang*
74) *Odyssey*
75) *Clyde*
76) *Nation*
77) *Dandy*
78) true
79) *17 Again*
80) J
81) K
82) three
83) *Full-Court Miracle*
84) *Cadet Kelly*
85) *Halloweentown II: Kalabar's Revenge*
86) *The Luck of the Irish*
87) *Phantom of the Megaplex*
88) *Zenon: Girl of the 21st Century*
89) *Harriet the Spy: Blog Wars*
90) *16 Wishes*
91) *Den Brother*

92) *Phineas and Ferb The Movie; Across the 2nd Dimension*

93) *Full House* (192)

94) *Star Trek: The Next Generation* (178)

95) *The Waltons* (213)

96) *King of the Hill* (255)

97) true

98) a

99) false

100) true

101) false

102) Orange County

103) Entertainment and Sports Programming Network

104) Cable News Network

105) Turner Classic Movies

106) Columbia Broadcasting System

107) 1 c, 2 b, 3 a, 4 e, 5 d

108) 1 b, 2 d, 3 c, 4 a

109) true

110) d

111) true

112) b

113) c

114) d

115) 1 c, 2 b, 3 a, 4 d, 5 e, 6 f

116) false

117) *Nacho Libre*

118) Bonds, Ruth, Sosa, McGwire, Maris

119) b

120) b

121) a

122) a

123) true

124) c

125) a perfect game

126) true–Henry Louis

127) 1 b, 2 d, 3 a, 4 e, 5 c

128) 1 b, 2 d, 3 c, 4 a

129) false

130) yes

131) yes

132) no
133) no
134) no
135) yes
136) yes
137) yes
138) no
139) yes
140) d
141) b
142) Babe Ruth, Mickey
     Mantle, Willie Stargell,
     Reggie Jackson
143) b
144) c
145) d
146) a
147) true
148) a
149) a
150) d
151) d
152) Don Newcombe
153) a
154) c

155) c
156) true
157) false
158) true
159) a
160) LaRussa, Cox, Torre,
     Anderson, Durocher
161) c
162) c
163) b
164) b
165) c
166) a
167) 1 a, 2 c, 3 d, 4 b
168) d
169) c
170) Dallas Cowboys
171) Cincinnati Bengals
172) Pittsburgh Steelers
173) New England Patriots
174) San Francisco 49ers
175) St. Louis Rams
176) Denver Broncos
177) Baltimore Ravens
178) San Diego Chargers

179) Tampa Bay Buccaneers
180) Jacksonville Jaguars
181) Los Angeles Rams
182) Detroit Lions
183) Buffalo Bills
184) Kansas City Chiefs
185) St. Louis Cardinals
186) Chicago Bears
187) Indianapolis Colts
188) Miami Dolphins
189) Atlanta Falcons
190) New York Jets
191) New York Giants
192) Cleveland Browns
193) Green Bay Packers
194) Washington Redskins
195) New Orleans Saints
196) true
197) false
198) center
199) true
200) b
201) guard
202) Detroit Pistons
203) b

204) false
205) true
206) false
207) None
208) Bill Bradley
209) false
210) false
211) false
212) false-it's in Spain
213) true
214) c
215) true
216) b
217) Ajax
218) 1 a, 2 d, 3 e, 4 b, 5 c, 6 f
219) c
220) Madison Square Garden
221) Mario Lemieux
222) d
223) a
224) lightweight
225) true
226) true

227) false-It became one in 1904
228) featherweight
229) true
230) false
231) d
232) false-that's a popular myth
233) c
234) a
235) a
236) there is no maximum-the ball must be holed
237) false
238) fourteen
239) no
240) there is no maximum number
241) no
242) the one farthest from the hole
243) no
244) you can either play it where it lies or take the shot over again
245) yes
246) true
247) b
248) c
249) false-with feathers
250) August
251) d
252) c
253) b
254) a
255) Arnold Palmer
256) b
257) Augusta, Georgia
258) d
259) green
260) eagle
261) albatross
262) double bogey
263) triple bogey
264) skins game

265) Jean van de Velde
266) Greg Norman
267) Jack Nicklaus
268) Lee Trevino
269) Michelle Wie
270) Annika Sorenstam
271) a
272) a
273) true
274) Coke
275) Coke
276) Coke
277) Pepsi
278) Pepsi
279) Coke
280) Pepsi
281) Coke
282) true
283) true
284) true
285) true-it produces
syrup for the
bottlers, who
produce the soda

286) Caffeine-Free Coca-
Cola
287) lemon
288) true
289) false-not until 1894
290) true
291) true
292) a
293) b
294) false-not until the
1950s
295) true
296) b
297) a
298) true
299) d
300) b
301) a
302) false-it happened in
1928
303) cherry
304) false-that was only
a marketing-created
story

305) true
306) false-although he did do ads for it
307) true
308) 3 Musketeers
309) Mars
310) c
311) c
312) a
313) Doublemint
314) a
315) d
316) c
317) c
318) true
319) false-it was named after New York City's Waldorf Hotel
320) c
321) d
322) d
323) China
324) c
325) b
326) true
327) false
328) corn
329) cheese
330) false-the term actually comes from "frijoles refritos" or "well-fried beans"
331) no
332) true
333) b
334) Beijing
335) d
336) c
337) true-Walter Payton
338) a
339) false
340) Michael Jordan
341) Toucan
342) 1 e, 2 d, 3 a, 4 c, 5 b, 6 f, 7 g
343) d
344) *Moby-Dick*
345) July 11

346) true-Kentucky
347) a bell
348) hush puppies
349) true
350) true
351) false
352) false
353) true
354) before
355) red and white
356) true
357) true
358) true
359) orange
360) restaurants
361) a weathervane
362) true
363) false
364) false-but it can be
used to shine copper
365) false-1951
366) 1 c, 2 b, 3 d, 4 a
367) blue
368) Reese's Pieces

369) Butterfinger
370) true
371) false-it was sold
for about 20 years
without one
372) b
373) c
374) false
375) b
376) a
377) c-but that was for
cooking, not eating
378) b
379) false
380) d
381) false-it was introduced
by New Yorker George
T. French at the 1904
St. Louis World's Fair
382) salt-water
383) false
384) false

385) false-it's named for founder George W. Church
386) true
387) c
388) b
389) b
390) true
391) elephant
392) Jean Lafoote
393) d
394) b
395) d
396) prunes
397) papaya
398) red pepper
399) onion
400) peas
401) c
402) three
403) five
404) true
405) false
406) seven
407) six
408) twelve
409) true
410) false-they're numbered
411) twelve
412) false-it was 300,000
413) true
414) false-pips
415) sixty-four
416) backgammon
417) red
418) red
419) Cadoo
420) true
421) false
422) presidential politics
423) Turn Crank
424) the marble
425) false
426) b
427) d
428) c
429) a twenty-sided dice
430) nine

431) false-it was Lexico
432) true
433) true
434) true
435) Us
436) Gs
437) yes
438) five
439) blue
440) true
441) b
442) d
443) false-it's Jake the
Jailbird
444) false
445) true
446) c
447) no
448) no
449) b
450)
451) Thirty-two
452) blue
453) white

454) yes
455) c
456) true
457) nothing-you aren't
allowed to do it
(banks can't go to
jail!)
458) two
459) false
460) States Avenue
461) Ventnor Ave.
462) true
463) a question mark
464) c
465) false-it was a London
mapmaker
466) true
467) false-King Carlos V
did, too
468) three

469) false-the first is three-on-three, the second is one-on-one, and the third is two-on-two, with no player playing more than twice.
470) fifteen
471) false-it was the Magnavox Odyssey
472) false-it's a term used when playing Go
473) c
474) b
475) Asteroids
476) a
477) Tetris
478) b
479) false-it was 1994, the same year that the Sony PlayStation was launched in Japan
480) d-and it was reached by a player in 1999
481) Tamagotchi
482) Sony PSP
483) true
484) Super Mario Bros. 3
485) Apple II
486) false-Playstation 2
487) b
488) c
489) pink and blue
490) Myst
491) true
492) yellow
493) SimCity
494) true
495) true
496) true
497) Simlish
498) The Sims: Hot Date
499) Pac-Man
500) Wii Fit
501) Tomb Raider II
502) Grand Theft Auto III
503) true
504) b

505) false-just white
506) Wii Play
507) Challenge
508) Monster
509) Lanes
510) Grade
511) Sluggers,
512) Bold
513) Academy
514) Rock
515) Hunter
516) Ops
517) Showdown
518) Rescue
519) Beat
520) Party
521) Dreamland
522) Sword
523) Olympic
524) Heroes
525) Doctor
526) Ninjas
527) d
528) c

529) Madden NFL 07
530) Brunswick Pro Bowling
531) LEGO Star Wars: The
    Complete Saga
532) LEGO Batman
533) b
534) Pigs
535) Red
536) Three
537) Eggs
538) twenty-one
539) true
540) b
541) cake
542) true
543) eight
544) a
545) true
546) Metroid games
547) Sonic the Hedgehog
    games
548) Batman games
549) Zelda games
550) Mario games

551) the mantle
552) d
553) c
554) true
555) d
556) d
557) a
558) b
559) Priscoan-between 4.6 and 3.8 billion years ago
560) true
561) a
562) true
563) sodium
564) potassium
565) silicon
566) true
567) c
568) b
569) ten
570) c
571) true
572) b
573) Australia
574) veldt
575) d
576) true
577) medium
578) small
579) false-Everest was a British surveyor
580) c
581) Pacific
582) over
583) more
584) less
585) less
586) c
587) b
588) true
589) c
590) true
591) c
592) c
593) d
594) true
595) growing

596) false-It's a flood level that has a one-percent chance of being matched or exceeded in a given year
597) Florida
598) New Jersey
599) Hawaii
600) North Carolina
601) California
602) false
603) Hawaii
604) Florida
605) Texas
606) California
607) Maine
608) Oregon
609) b
610) longer
611) true
612) false
613) the Amazon

614) false-the Amazon can grow to be just over 20 miles wide
615) true
616) c
617) east
618) true
619) sound
620) true-multiple times
621) Nepal
622) true
623) South America
624) Australia
625) Europe
626) North America
627) Asia
628) *Snow White and the Seven Dwarfs, Pinocchio, Fantasia, Dumbo, Bambi*
629) Cogsworth
630) chop wood
631) expectorating
632) Mrs. Potts

633) false-it lost to
   Silence of the Lambs
634) blue
635) true
636) twice
637) twenty-first
638) b
639) "Under the Sea"
640) Scuttle the seagull
641) three
642) a fork
643) false
644) Vanessa
645) Timothy
646) true
647) no
648) false-Drizella and
   Anastasia
649) true
650) "The Second Star to
   the Right"
651) left
652) spaghetti and
   meatballs

653) true
654) Italian
655) the hound
656) fox
657) three
658) true-It was Phil
   Harris
659) true
660) b
661) false
662) b
663) d
664) Zeus
665) five
666) true
667) false
668) b
669) *Late Night with David
   Letterman*
670) 1,000 BC
671) Pegasus
672) true-Victor and Hugo
   are named for Victor
   Hugo

673) "God Help the
     Outcasts"
674) true
675) *Wicked*
676) true
677) false
678) true-it was Matthew
     Broderick
679) *Star Wars*-he voiced
Darth Vader
680) Mice
681) *101 Dalmatians*
682) *The Princess and the
     Frog*
683) *The Hunchback of
     Notre Dame*
684) *Beauty and the Beast*
685) *Hercules*
686) *Aladdin*
687) *The Rescuers*
688) *Sleeping Beauty*
689) *Bambi*
690) *Pocahontas*
691) *The Great Mouse
     Detective*

692) *The Lion King*
693) *Mulan*
694) *The Jungle Book*
695) *Pinocchio*
696) *Oliver and Company*
697) *The Little Mermaid*
698) Siamese
699) Darling
700) his shadow
701) Princess Aurora
702) Mufasa
703) Simba
704) fox
705) Timothy
706) Eric
707) Philip
708) Prince Charming
709) Phoebus
710) Aladdin
711) Hercules
712) Simba
713) John Smith
714) Naveen
715) Robin Hood